100 E
Food Recipes

By Lev Well

ISBN: 1530262216
ISBN-13: 978-1530262212

CONTENTS:

3

4

Beverages

Almond Shrub

INGREDIENTS:
1 glass orange juice
1 quart rum
rind of 1 lemons
1/2 lb sugar
1 glass milk
5 - 10 drops almond extract

INSTRUCTIONS:
Put into jar the rum. Add thin lemon rind, orange juice, and sugar. Add the essence of bitter almonds to the glass of milk. Mix the milk thoroughly and add to the jar. Cover the jar and put it in a warm place (65-70°F). Keep until the milk has curdled (1-3 hours. Filter through filter paper and bottle. Leave it for 2 weeks before drinking.

Almond Shrub Spritzer

INGREDIENTS:
1 oz Almond Shrub (see recipe)
8 oz Sparkling Water or Seltzer (see NOTE)
lemon or lime slices

INSTRUCTIONS:
In cocktail glass combine all ingredients. Mix thoroughly. Add ice. Garnish the drink with lemon or lime slices. Enjoy.

NOTE: For a sweeter drink use ginger ale or 7-up instead the water.

Bloody Mary #1

INGREDIENTS:
1 1/2 oz vodka
3 oz tomato juice
1/2 oz lemon juice

7 drops Worcestershire sauce
3 drops Tabasco sauce
freshly ground pepper
1 dash celery salt, freshly grated

INSTRUCTIONS:
Combine ingredients in glass filled with ice. Stir gently. Serve the
Bloody Mary in a pint glass. Garnish with a stalk of celery, pickled
asparagus.

Source: "DavisWiki.org"

Bloody Mary #2

INGREDIENTS:
1 quart Beefamato or Clamato juice
Juice of one lemon
1 teaspoon Worcestershire sauce
1 teaspoon Tabasco brand hot sauce
1 tablespoon prepared horseradish
1/4 teaspoon garlic salt
1/4 teaspoon celery salt
Freshly ground white pepper
1 and 1/2 cups pepper-flavored or plain vodka
Lemon or lime slices for garnish

INSTRUCTIONS:
Mix all ingredients in a 2-quart pitcher. Stir until well blended. Pour into
ice-filled glasses, and garnish with lemon or lime. Or a stalk of celery!

Makes 6 to 8 servings.

Source: "DavisWiki.org"

Brunch Punch

INGREDIENTS:
1 (12-ounce) can frozen orange juice concentrate, thawed

1 (12-ounce) can frozen lemonade concentrate, thawed
3 cups pineapple juice
2 cups peach nectar
1 (1-liter) bottle ginger ale
5 cups ice cubes

For garnish:
Orange, lemon, and pineapple slices

INSTRUCTIONS:
Add to a large punch dish the orange juice, lemonade concentrates, pineapple juice and peach nectar. Mix well. Cover the bowl and cool before serving. Then blend in ginger ale. Add ice cubes. Put fruit slices on top, and serve.

Serves 15.

Notes: If you prefer an alcoholic version, substitute 1 (750-ml) bottle of champagne for the ginger ale.

Champagne Shrub

INGREDIENTS:
1 oz raspberry rhrub (see recipe)
4 oz champagne
4 oz ginger ale

INSTRUCTIONS:
Pour the liquids into a glass in the following sequence: first - the shrub, then champagne and after that - the ginger ale. Stir the mix thoroughly. Serve immediately.

Dark Chocolate Cinnamon Easter Eggnog

INGREDIENTS:
4 egg yolks
2 cups milk
cup granulated sugar

1/4 cup finely chopped dark chocolate
2 tablespoons unsweetened dark cocoa powder
1/4 teaspoon cinnamon
1 cup heavy whipping cream
1/4 cup chocolate liqueur (such as Godiva Original Liqueur)
1 teaspoon vanilla
Garnish (optional): whipped cream and cinnamon

INSTRUCTIONS:
In a medium saucepan over medium heat, whisk together egg yolks, milk, sugar, dark chocolate, cocoa powder, and cinnamon. When mixture is well combined and just starts to boil and bubble, remove from heat.

Pour mixture in a bowl over an ice bath and whisk for several minutes until cool. Whisk in cream, liqueur, and vanilla. Serve immediately or store in refrigerator.

Top with whipped cream and cinnamon if desired.

Yield: 4 drinks

SNAPPY TIP: Make sure you whisk the egg yolks and liquids well while over the heat so that the eggs don't curdle.

SNAPPY SUBSTITUTIONS: If you don't like dark chocolate you could use original unsweetened cocoa powder, and substitute your favorite chopped chocolate for the chopped dark chocolate. You can also substitute any liqueur for the chocolate liqueur.

Source: "Foodista.com – The Cooking Encyclopedia Everyone Can Edit".

Ginger Shrub

INGREDIENTS:
1/2 cup ginger, finely minced
1 cup apple cider vinegar
1/2 cup sugar

INSTRUCTIONS:

Put the ginger and the vinegar in a saucepan. Heat over high heat until the mixture begins to boil just around the edges. Pour into a glass jar and cool. Cover and let it steep at room temperature for 24 hours.

Strain the mixture and put the liquid in a saucepan. Add in the sugar. Bring to a boil over medium heat. Reduce to low heat and simmer a few minutes, stirring occasionally.

Cool the shrub syrup and store in the refrigerator. Serve diluted to taste (generally 1:10) with water, juice, soda water or lemonade.

Orange Shrub

INGREDIENTS:
2 quart rum
6 oranges
1 pint orange juice
1 pint cold water
2-3 lb sugar

INSTRUCTIONS:
Peel oranges and place the pare into a jar. Add to the jar the juice of these oranges. Add water and close the jar. Leave to stay for 3 days, stirring occasionally. Strain into a pan. Add sugar and bring to boil. Add a pint of orange juice, stir and strain again. Add rum, stir and bottle.

Orange Shrub Spritzer

INGREDIENTS:
1 oz Orange Shrub (see recipe)
8 oz Sparkling Water or Seltzer (see NOTE)
lemon or lime slices

INSTRUCTIONS:
In cocktail glass combine all ingredients. Mix thoroughly. Add ice. Garnish the drink with lemon or lime slices. Enjoy.

NOTE: For a sweeter drink use ginger ale or 7-up instead the water.

Raspberry Shrub

INGREDIENTS:
4 quarts raspberries
1 quart raspberry vinegar (see recipe)

INSTRUCTIONS:
Mix vinegar and berries and leave the mix stay for 4 days at home temperature. Strain the mixture. Add 2 cups of sugar to each pint of liquid. Boil about 20 minutes. Bottle the shrub and keep in a cool place. Serve adding 1 tablespoon of the shrub to a glass of water.

White Wine Spritzer

INGREDIENTS:
1 oz Orange Shrub (see recipe)
4 oz White Wine
5 oz Sparkling Water or Seltzer

INSTRUCTIONS:
In cocktail glass combine all ingredients. Mix thoroughly. Add ice. Garnish the drink with fresh fruits.

Appetizers and Salads

Chutney Deviled Eggs

INGREDIENTS:
6 hard-boiled eggs
2-3 tablespoons mayonnaise
1 teaspoon Dijon mustard
1 tablespoon Rhubarb Chutney (see recipe)
pinch of sea salt
paprika

2 tablespoons finely chopped parsley

INSTRUCTIONS:
Peel hard-boiled eggs. Cut them in halves longwise.

Take out the yolks into a small bowl. Add to this bowl mayonnaise, Dijon mustard, chutney, salt. Mix well.

With a teaspoon put small amounts of the yolk mixture evenly back into egg halves. Sprinkle the eggs with paprika and garnish with chopped parsley.

Serves 6.

Corn Salad and Avocado Salad with Lemon Vinaigrette

INGREDIENTS:
6-8 oz corn salad
Sliced avocadoes
Radish Roses for garnish (one per plate)
Lemon Vinaigrette (see recipe)

INSTRUCTIONS:
On plates, make a nest of corn salad. Arrange the avocado slices in a flower pattern. Place a radish rose in the center. Drizzle with Lemon vinaigrette.

Serves 4-6.

Ginger Glazed Carrots

INGREDIENTS:
3 cups cooked carrots, julienne
3 tablespoons Ginger Shrub (see recipe)
1 tablespoon butter

INSTRUCTIONS:

Put butter and Ginger Shrub in a sauté pan. Heat over medium heat stirring until hot and bubbly. Add carrots and sauté until nicely glazed.

Serves 6.

Greek Vegetable Salad

INGREDIENTS:
1/2 head romaine lettuce
2 cups Chopped tomatoes
1 Cucumber, thinly sliced
1 small Onion, sliced or chopped
1 Green bell pepper, chopped
3 ounces Feta cheese, crumbled
4 tablespoons Red wine vinegar
2 teaspoons Olive oil
1 tablespoon Water
1 Clove garlic, crushed
Black pepper

INSTRUCTIONS:
In a large bowl, toss lettuce, tomato, cucumber, onion, and green pepper.

Top with cheese. In a separate bowl, whisk oil, vinegar, water, garlic, and pepper. Pour over salad and toss.

Serves 4.

Source: "Foodista.com – The Cooking Encyclopedia Everyone Can Edit".

Ham Pie

INGREDIENTS:
Two 9-inch pastry crusts
8 oz. thin sliced ham
5 oz. frozen spinach, thawed
3 eggs (room temperature)

2 cups shredded Mozzarella cheese
15 oz. Ricotta cheese
1 small red bell pepper, thinly sliced
1 tablespoon olive oil
1 tablespoon chopped basil leaves
Lemon pepper to taste

INSTRUCTIONS:
Heat up oven to 345°F. Line baking dish with first pie crust. In the skillet saute peppers and ham in olive oil for 3 minutes. Pepper. In large bowl beat 2 eggs and ricotta. Spread mixture onto the crust. Pat dry spinach and spread it on the top of mixture. Sprinkle peppers and ham over spinach and top with first mozzarella and then basil leaves. Put on the top the second pie crust and trim the edges. Cut vents in top of crust and brush the top crust with 1 beaten egg. Bake 50-60 minutes, or until golden brown. Cool about 15 minutes before serving.

Italian Roasted Vegetables

INGREDIENTS:
2 Yellow Peppers sliced
2 Red Bell Peppers sliced
2 Green Peppers sliced
3 Zucchini Sliced Lengthwise
2 Japanese Eggplant Sliced
24 spears Asparagus Whole, trimmed
1 pound Baby New Potatoes Sliced thin
8 ounces Mushrooms Halved or whole
1 sprig Fresh Rosemary Chopped
12 cloves Garlic Chopped
1/4 cup Extra Virgin olive oil
Salt and pepper To taste

INSTRUCTIONS:
Preheat oven to 400°F. Put veggies into open roasting pan. Toss with rosemary, chopped garlic, salt and fresh ground black pepper and just enough olive oil to coat. Roast for about 30-45 minutes, or until fork-tender.

NOTE: Serve hot or at room temperature with fresh Italian bread.

Jambon Persille

Serve with a Beaujolais nouveau or at Easter (the traditional time to eat this dish) a Beaujolais villages.

INGREDIENTS:
1 small uncooked salted ham about 3.5kg or 1 uncooked salted shoulder of ham about 2.5kg
200 grams carrots
150 grams onions stuck with 3 cloves
1 large bouquet garni with plenty of thyme
1 tablespoon crushed peppercorns
shin of veal blanched
1 calfs foot split lengthways and blached
1 bottle white burgundy (Aligote SaintVeran or Macon)
1 tablespoon good wine vinegar
150 grams shallots finely chopped
20 grams garlic finely chopped
3 tablespoons snipped flat leaved parsley
1 tablespoon snipped tarragon
2 tablespoons chervil leaves (1 for preparing the terrines 1 for the moulds)
1 salt and freshly ground pepper

INSTRUCTIONS:
Soak the ham or shoulder under a trickle of cold running water for 12-24 hours to remove the salt. Place in a large pan and cover with fresh cold water. Bring gently to simmering point; if possible use a thermometer to check the temperature reaches 80 to 90°C (175 to 195°F) maximum.

Cook very gently for 30 minutes skimming the surface as often as possible then add the carrots, onions, bouquet garni, peppercorns, shin of veal and the calfs foot. Simmer for a further 2 hours then pour in 650ml white wine and cook for another 30 minutes.

The ham or shoulder should now be so well cooked that you can shred it with a fork. Leave in the pan to cool to 30°C (85°F). Remove the meat from the pan and discard all the aromatics. Strain the cooking liquid through a conical sieve into a saucepan. Skim off the fat and boil to reduce by half.

Take the pan off the heat and stir in the vinegar. Pour the liquid into a bowl set on crushed ice and leave to cool to a jelly stirring with a spatula from time to time. Season.

While the jelly is cooling take the meat off the bones of the calfs foot shin of veal and ham. Discard some of the rind and fat then cut the shin and ham into large cubes and the calfs foot into very small dice.

Pour the rest of the wine into a saucepan. Add the chopped shallots and cook for 3 minutes. Take the pan off the heat, add the garlic then pour into a chilled bowl and leave to cool.

When the liquid is cold add the chopped parsley and tarragon, 1 tablespoon chervil and the diced calfs foot. Take the terrines or ham dishes out of the fridge and line the bottom and sides of each with a thin layer of half-set jelly.

Make a layer of large cubes of veal and ham then pour on a little more half-set jelly. Spoon in some of the diced calfs foot and herb mixture pour on a little more jelly then make another layer of cubed veal and ham. Make 3 or 4 layers in this way ending with a thin even layer of jelly.

Delicately press some chervil leaves into this layer then refrigerate the terrines for at least 12 hours.

Serve the ham in the terrine and give your guests a large flat knife (such as a boning or charcuterie knife) to cut their own portion. Cut off the first outside slice before presenting the terrine at table.

Serve with Dijon mustard, homepickled gherkins and small white onions in vinegar and salad of dandelion leaves with garlic croutons.

NOTE: This dish will keep very well in the fridge for several days so it is worth making a couple of terrines at the same time.

Makes 2 terrines to serve 20 people.

Peppers Stuffed with Cheese and Eggs

INGREDIENTS:
3 bell peppers (preferably different colors)
300-400 g of cheese grated
3 eggs hard boiled and peeled
2-3 cloves of garlic minced
mayonnaise

INSTRUCTIONS:
In bowl combine cheese and stir. Add a little mayonnaise, mix well.

Wash peppers and remove seeds. Stuff peppers with cheese mixture, leaving the place in the middle for egg. Put an egg in the middle of the pepper and fill in the free space of pepper with cheese mixture.

Place the peppers in the refrigerator for 3-4 hours. Then with a sharp knife cut the bells into slices and serve.

Slovak Sirok

It is a traditional Slovak Easter food.

INGREDIENTS:
15 eggs lightly beaten
1 quart milk
salt to taste
black pepper to taste

INSTRUCTIONS:
Pour milk in a pan. Bring the milk to boil. Slowly add eggs to the milk. Salt and pepper. Cook stirring constantly.

When all the eggs are cooked, pour mixture into a linen towel, squeeze the mixture into a ball shape in the towel and tie. Hang over sink and drain for several hours. Remove from the towel and refrigerate.

Tomato Slices Stuffed With Egg

INGREDIENTS:
4 tomatoes, sliced
4 boiled eggs, finely chopped
150 grams white cheese, grated
4 tablespoons mayonnaise
3 tablespoons sour cream
Salt, pepper to taste

INSTRUCTIONS:
In a bowl combine egg, cheese, mayonnaise and sour cream. Season with salt and pepper.

On a plate arrange slices of tomato. Top with egg mixture, about 1 tablespoon per slice.

Serves 4.

Source: "Foodista.com – The Cooking Encyclopedia Everyone Can Edit".

Tortellini Salad with Fresh Herbs

INGREDIENTS:
1 package (10-ounce) cheese tortellini (about 3 cups)
1 1/2 tablespoons extra-virgin olive oil
1 tablespoon tarragon vinegar
1 tablespoon finely chopped fresh tarragon
1/2 teaspoon sea salt
Dash black pepper
1 red pepper, finely diced
2 mediums carrots, peeled and grated

1 medium zucchini, grated
1 tablespoon finely chopped fresh parsley

INSTRUCTIONS:
Cook tortellini per package instructions. (Fresh tortellini takes 6-8 minutes to cook.)

Drain and run under cold water to stop it from cooking. Set aside to cool further.

In a large bowl, whisk together olive oil, tarragon vinegar, chopped tarragon, salt and pepper.

Stir in the vegetables and the cooked tortellini.

When everything is well combined, taste, and add salt and pepper, if needed.

Sprinkle parsley over pasta and vegetables, and stir gently until combined.

Refrigerate for as little as an hour or as long as overnight, or serve immediately.

Serves 4.

Source: "Foodista.com – The Cooking Encyclopedia Everyone Can Edit".

Warm Brie with Honey-Fig Jam and Pecans

INGREDIENTS:
1 small round of brie
4 oz Honey-Fig Jam (see recipe)
1/2 cup chopped pecans
crackers or sliced baguette

INSTRUCTIONS:

Place the round of brie in a small, shallow baking dish. Top with the Honey-Fig Jam. Bake for 15 minutes at 350°F. Sprinkle with the pecans. Serve with crackers or sliced baguette.

Serves 6

Soups

Barszcz - Polish Borsch (Polish Easter Soup)

INGREDIENTS:
6 cups water
1 pound Polish kielbasa sausage
2 cups sour cream
Salt and freshly ground pepper, to taste
1 tablespoon plain or beet horseradish
2 tablespoons lemon juice or vinegar, or to taste
1 cup sliced mushrooms
6 hard boiled eggs, peeled and sliced
1 cup cubed, cooked ham
1 cup cooked diced potatoes
1 cup cooked diced beets (optional)
Chopped fresh dill or parsley (for garnish)

INSTRUCTIONS:
Pour water into a large kettle. Bring water to a boil. Add the kielbasa and cook for 1 hour until it is well cooked.

Remove kielbasa from water and cut into thin slices. Add to the broth the horseradish, mushrooms, salt and pepper and simmer covered for about 15 minutes. Set aside to cool.

In another bowl, beat sour cream with about 3 cups of the cool broth. Pour this mixture back into the kettle with the rest of the broth. Add lemon juice or vinegar.

Put in the individual serving bowls thinly sliced kielbasa pieces, hard boiled eggs, ham, potatoes or beets to taste. Reheat the broth in the kettle before serving, but do NOT bring to a boil. Pour broth into individual serving bowls.

The broth may be made a day or two before and kept refrigerated.

Serves 4 to 6.

Bavarian Herb Soup

INGREDIENTS:
1 lb herbs (see NOTE)
4 tablespoons butter
1 large onion, chopped
1 quart water (or vegetable stock - see recipe)
1 large potato, peeled and chopped into small cubes
salt and pepper
bread cubes for croutons

INSTRUCTIONS:
Take a large saucepan. Wash the herbs and strip the leaves from those stalks which are too woody. Cut fine the rest.

In a deep pan with melted butter fry the onion until transparent. Add the herbs and pour in the water or broth. Add the potato. Bring the soup to boil, and lower the heat. Simmer the soup for 20 minutes. Puree the potato in the soup to thicken it a little. Salt and pepper to taste.

Serve the soup with hot bread croutons fried in butter or bacon fat (goose fat is even better).

Serves 4.

NOTE: Use at least 3 of these: chervil, watercress, spinach, sorrel (also dandelion and pimpernel for brave souls). Bitter herbs are traditionally eaten at Easter in Christian countries as a sign of penitence. This Bavarian soup is served on Easter Thursday, known as Maundy Thursday. Fresh chervil, easily available in any German market, is usually the dominating flavor. This is a delicate fresh-tasting soup for any time of the year.

Easter Lettuce Soup

INGREDIENTS:
1/2 pound veal
1 whole chicken breast, boned and skinned
4 tablespoons (1/2 stick) butter
Salt
Black pepper, ground fresh
1 1/2 tablespoons chopped onion
1 tablespoon carrot chopped very fine
2 tablespoons fresh ricotta
1/2 cup freshly grated parmesan cheese, plus additional amount of cheese for each serving
1 teaspoon fresh marjoram OR 3/4 teaspoon dried
1 tablespoon chopped parsley
1 egg yolk
3 heads Boston lettuce
4 cups meat broth
For each serving: 1 slice of bread toasted dark or browned in butter

INSTRUCTIONS:
Slice the veal and the chicken into 1-inch pieces.

Preheat all the butter in a large sauté pan. Put in the veal, a 1-2 pinches of salt and 1-2 grindings of pepper.
Cook turning the veal until brown evenly on all sides. Remove the veal to a plate.

Place the chicken pieces in the pan. Add a little salt and pepper. Cook a little, just until the meat loses its uncooked shine. Remove the chicken to the plate with the veal.

Put the onion into the pan and cook stirring until goldish. Add the celery and carrot and cook stirring occasionally until the vegetables are tender. Pour the vegetables together with all the juices in the pan into a bowl.

Chop very fine (or mince) the cooked veal and chicken. Add the meat to the bowl.

Put into the bowl the ricotta, parmesan, the marjoram, parsley and egg yolk. Mix thoroughly until all ingredients are smoothly blended. Taste and correct for salt and pepper.

Discard the bad outer leaves of the lettuce. Pull off all the others and rinse them in cold water. But save the very small leaves to use on another occasion in a salad.

Bring 1 gallon of water to a boil. Add 1 tablespoon of salt, put in 3 or 4 lettuce leaves and retrieve them after 5 or 6 seconds.

Spread the leaves on a work area. Cut away any hard part of the central rib. On each leaf, place 1 tablespoon of the mixture from the bowl in the shape of a narrow sausage. Wrap the leaf around the stuffing. Squeeze each leaf in your hand to tighten the wrapping, and set it aside.

Repeat the above procedure with the remaining leaves. When the leaves get smaller, slightly overlap 2 of them to make a single wrapper.

When you stuffed all the leaves, put them side by side in a large saucepan. Don't leave space between them, and make as many layers as necessary.
Take a dinner plate small enough to fit inside the pan and place it on the top layer of the lettuce rolls to keep them in place while cooking.

Pour enough broth in the saucepan to cover the plate inside by about 1 inch. Cover the pot and simmer for 30 minutes.

Meanwhile pour the remaining broth into a small saucepan, cover, and turn and heat on low heat.

When the lettuce rolls are done, transfer them to individual plates or bowls onto a single slice of toasted or browned bread. Pour over them any of the broth remaining in the larger pot and all the hot broth from the small saucepan. Sprinkle grated Parmesan over each plate and serve immediately.

Serves 4-6.

Easter Potato Soup

INGREDIENTS:
2 cup sour cream
3/2 pound cooked ham
5 large potatoes peeled
3/2 pound cooked Polish sausage
2 quarts buttermilk
Salt and pepper to taste
2 tablespoon flour mixed with water
4 tablespoons grated horseradish
10 eggs hard-boiled, peeled and sliced

INSTRUCTIONS:
Warm buttermilk on rather low heat until cheese sets on top. Cool-down and strain in a fine strainer. Put the whey aside.

Boil potatoes in 10 cups of water. When the potatoes are tender, add sliced sausage, diced ham, whey and horseradish. Bring the mixture to a boil and add flour. Add sour cream and boil for 3 minutes.

Garnish the soup with sliced eggs and serve.

Greek Easter Soup with Avgolemeno Sauce

INGREDIENTS:
For broth:
1/2 chicken, cut up
3 cups water
1/2 cup (1 stick) butter
4 scallions, finely chopped
5 cups water or chicken consomme
1/2 cup fresh dill
1/2 cup parsley, finely chopped
1/2 cup rice
Salt and pepper

For Avgolemeno Sauce (Egg-Lemon Sauce):
7 eggs (at room temperature)
2 tablespoons water
Juice of 3 lemons

INSTRUCTIONS:
Prepare Broth:
Boil chicken in the 3 cups water for 50 minutes. Remove from heat; strain broth and set aside. Chop chicken into pieces. Cook onion, dill and parsley in butter with 1 teaspoon salt and a dash of pepper until soft and transparent (be careful not to brown). Add chopped chicken and cook over moderate heat for about 5 minutes, stirring frequently. Add chicken broth and enough water to make 2 quarts liquid. Bring to boil and add rice. Reduce heat and cook until rice is done. Remove the soup from heat.

Prepare Avgolemeno Sauce:
Beat egg whites with water until stiff. Blend in egg yolks, then add lemon juice, beating until thick. With a ladle, add a small amount of hot broth to the egg mixture, blending quickly.

Pour Avgolemeno sauce into the soup, blend and serve immediately.

Ham Soup

INGREDIENTS:
1 tablespoon olive oil
1 cup sweet onion, small diced
1 medium carrot, small diced
2 cloves of garlic, minced
Pinch of salt and pepper
1/2 cup red wine
1 cup chard, chiffonade
1 cup of finely diced ham (or more to your liking)
1 cup canned diced tomatoes
1 cup canned beans,
3 cups beef stock (or other stock)
1 pinch chili powder
white cheddar (optional)

INSTRUCTIONS:
Add one tablespoon of olive oil to a pot over medium heat. When oil is hot, add onions, carrots and garlic and stir frequently. Add a pinch of salt and pepper and stir. Cook for 3 minutes, continuing to stir. Reduce heat if your pan begins to smoke. Add red wine and stir. Cook for an additional 2-3 minutes. Add chard and ham and cook for another 4 minutes, allowing the ham's juices to release, add tomatoes and canned beans and stir. Add stock and chili powder and stir. Cook for at least 5-10 minutes longer. Taste for seasonings and serve with slices

Source: "Foodista.com – The Cooking Encyclopedia Everyone Can Edit".

Lamb Soup

INGREDIENTS:
1 tablespoon olive oil
1 onion, finely chopped
4 cups chicken broth
1/2 pound boneless lamb, trimmed of excess fat and cut into 1/4- to 1/2-inch pieces
3/4 cups chopped fresh Italian parsley
1/4 cup chopped fresh dill
1/6 cup long-grain rice
2 egg yolks
1/4 cup fresh lemon juice
Salt and freshly ground pepper to taste

INSTRUCTIONS:
Preheat the olive oil in a large stockpot. Sauté onions for 4 minutes until tender.

Add to the pot chicken broth, lamb, parsley and dill. Bring to a boil. Lower heat, cover and simmer for about 50 minutes. Add rice and keep on simmering about 15 minutes until soft.

In a medium bowl combine the egg yolks and lemon juice. Beat until frothy. Gradually add 1 to 2 cups of hot soup to the yolks mixture, beating vigorously to preserve eggs from curdling.

Pour the yolks mixture back into the stockpot. Stir well. Serve.

Hot dishes

Beef Baked with Bacon and Herbs

INGREDIENTS:
1 kg of beef
9-12 Strips of bacon
9-12 sage leaves (or rosemary, or oregano)

For Marinade:
5 tablespoons vegetable oil
1 clove of garlic, crashed
1 tablespoon dried or fresh thyme
salt
pepper

INSTRUCTIONS:
To prepare the marinade combine in the bowl the vegetable oil, garlic, thyme, salt and pepper. Stir.

Cut the meat into pieces about 1 1/2 cm thick and roll in the marinade. Put in one layer on a baking dish. Put the sage leaves on the meat. Wrap each piece of meat with strips of bacon.

Place the baking dish in a preheated oven at 355°F (180°C) for about 1 hour.

Garnish with mashed potatoes or cooked rice.

Chicken Breast Stuffed with Ham and Spinach

INGREDIENTS:
2 (10-14 oz.) chicken breasts, boneless, skinless

6 ounces ham, boneless, fat removed
1 1/2 tablespoons butter or oil
1 tablespoon flour, all purpose
1/4 cup milk
4 ounces spinach, fresh, cleaned, blanched
1 1/2 tablespoons oil
1 tablespoon all-purpose flour
1 1/2 cups chicken stock
2 ounces onions, finely diced
1/2 ounce celery, fine bias cut
1/2 ounce carrots, fine bias cut
1 bay leaf
1 cup White wine
4 ounces heavy cream
Salt
White pepper

INSTRUCTIONS:
Prepare chicken breast as follows: Cut each breast in half, removing the joining cartilage. Remove the tenderloin from the breast and remove the tendon from the tenderloin. On a hard flat surface, preferably a cutting board, lay a piece of plastic wrap. Place the tenderloins on the wrap and fold wrap over to cover the tenderloins.

With a meat tenderizing mallet or a cleaver, gently flatten the tenderloins to 1/8-inch thickness. Repeat this procedure with all of the remaining chicken. Set aside for later use. (Refrigerate.)

Prepare stuffing as follows: Mince ham in food processor. Melt butter in small saucepan and add flour. Cook over medium heat for 2-3 minutes. DO NOT BROWN. Add milk, stirring constantly, and cook until thick paste forms. Add ham and remove from heat. Let cool. Reserve spinach for later use.

Stuff chicken breast as follows: Place 1 ounce of spinach on each of the chicken breasts, leaving 1 inch from all edges uncovered. Place 1 1/2 ounces of the ham mixture on top of each breast in the center and cover with each of the four tenderloins. Gently wrap ends of chicken breast towards the center, folding them over the tenderloins.

Carefully pick them up, invert them, and place them on a plate and shape them like a large Easter egg. After stuffing the breasts, place them in the freezer and allow them to set for easier handling (30-40 minutes).

Prepare sauce as follows: Place oil in a small saucepan and add vegetables and bay leaf. Cook 3-5 minutes over medium high heat. Add wine and reduce down until oil has a clear appearance. Add flour and continue to cook for 3-4 minutes, while stirring constantly. DO NOT BROWN.

Add hot chicken stock and stir. Bring to simmering point and add heavy cream. Adjust seasonings to your liking. Pass sauce through a strainer and keep warm until serving time.

Cook the chicken breasts as follows: Preheat oven to 350°F. Pour 1/4 inch oil in bottom of a heavy skillet and put on medium heat. Remove chicken from freezer and dredge in flour, dip in beaten egg and place in the skillet, with seam sides down. Brown lightly on all sides.

Place browned chicken breasts on the baking sheet pan and bake in oven for about 20 minutes, until chicken is done and stuffing is hot through. Serve with sauce.

Serves 4.

Source: "Foodista.com – The Cooking Encyclopedia Everyone Can Edit".

Chicken in Spicy Sauce

INGREDIENTS:
1 red bell pepper, cored and stripped of its seeds and sliced
4 onions chopped
1 garlic clove chopped
250g (1/2 lb) champignon mushrooms sliced
2 cups dry white wine
vegetable oil
paprika
salt

INSTRUCTIONS:
Cut chicken into serving pieces. Rub with salt paprika. Sear in oil.

Put in sauté pan onions and garlic. Pour wine. Put chicken pieces and pour on oil. Cover and cook 10-15 minutes. Add red pepper and mushrooms. Cook until the vegetables and chicken are tender.

Chicken Tenders with Yam Medallions

INGREDIENTS:
2 inches large boneless skinless chicken breasts, sliced into 1 thick tenders
2 large pre-baked yams
2 tablespoons butter
1 can pineapple chunks in natural juice
3 tablespoons brown sugar
1/4 cup vinegar
1 teaspoon cornstarch
Salt and pepper to taste
1/2 teaspoon garlic powder

INSTRUCTIONS:
First, bake the yams for 1 hour in a 350°F oven and cool completely. Peel the yams carefully, then slice them into 3/4 inch thick rounds.

In a saucepan, heat the pineapple with the juice, and the brown sugar until nearly boiling.

Mix the cornstarch with the vinegar until well-blended, then add to the hot liquid in the saucepan, stirring briskly as it thickens. Set aside.

In a large skillet, brown the chicken tenders in 1 tablespoon butter, sprinkling with salt, pepper, and garlic powder. When thoroughly cooked, set the chicken aside on a plate.

Using the same skillet, brown the yam medallions on both sides in the 2nd Tablespoon of butter.

Lay the chicken tenders on top of the yam medallions and pour the sauce over all. Cover and reduce heat to lowest setting for about 10 minutes to allow flavors to blend.

Serves 4.

Source: "Foodista.com – The Cooking Encyclopedia Everyone Can Edit".

Chicken With Grilled Onions and Sumac

INGREDIENTS:
3 pounds chicken breast boiled with a couple of Bay leaves, salt
3 onions, diced, seasoned and grilled
2 eggs for brushing the top of the dough
3 tea spoons of sumac seasoning
1 package puff pastry dough, about 12 large pieces
juice of one lemon
4 tablespoons of olive oil
Salt to taste
1 teaspoon paprika
teaspoon black pepper
Pickles or peppers for garnish

INSTRUCTIONS:
Boil the chicken (with seasonings) and shred. Combine chopped onions and 1/2 of the sumac seasoning and the olive oil in a saucepan; caramelize the onions. Add the remainder of the seasoning to the chicken. Combine chicken with onions and cook for about 5 minutes

Place chicken on the dough and fold to any shape you prefer. Press tight so chicken stays in. Brush with eggs.

Preheat oven to 375°F. Bake about 20 minutes, or until golden. Garnish with pickles or peppers.

NOTE: You can also use floor tortilla if you don't wish to use dough or you don't have it. Use same exact recipe, place on a tortilla and roll like a small burritos, don't forget to brush the top with eggs before you bake.

Chorizo and Cheese Crostini

INGREDIENTS:
1/4 head cabbage, grated
1/2 cup mixture of grated Muenster and Daisy cheese
1 pound cooked chorizo, casings removed
1/2 loaf of Italian baguette

INSTRUCTIONS:
Preheat oven to 400°F.

Heat a 12-inch cast-iron skillet. Add the chorizo, break it into chunks with a wooden spoon and cook over moderate heat, turning, until cooked through and lightly browned, about 8 minutes. Remove from heat to allow to cool. (This step can be done and advance and refrigerated overnight.)

Grate cheeses and cabbage.

Slice baguette into 1/4 inch slices on a slight diagonal angle. Place on a cooking sheet. (Consider lining with foil for easy clean-up since you will spoon the mixture on to each slice.)

Combine the cheese and cabbage with the cooked chorizo. Using a spoon, top each baguette slice with one or two spoonfuls.

Heat in the oven for 10 minutes to allow for cheese to melt and bread to get crispy.

Filet Mignon with Horseradish Gravy

INGREDIENTS:
1 (3/4-ounce) package brown gravy mix
2 tablespoons prepared horseradish
4 (5-ounce) beef tenderloin steaks
1/4 teaspoon salt
1/4 teaspoon black pepper
2 tablespoons butter
1 (8-ounce) package sliced fresh mushrooms

INSTRUCTIONS:
Make gravy according to package directions. Stir in horseradish. Set aside.

Melt butter in skillet over moderate heat. Add mushrooms, and cook, stirring constantly, 5 minutes or until tender. Take out from heat and stir in gravy.

Grease a large nonstick skillet with cooking spray. Put skillet over medium-high heat. Add steaks, and fry 1 minute on each side. (Steaks will be rare.) Place the stakes in a lightly greased 1-quart baking dish. Season with salt and balck pepper. Pour gravy over steaks.

Heat the oven to 340°F. Put baking dish into the oven and bake, uncovered, about 15 minutes or to desired degree of doneness. Serve with mashed potatoes and steamed asparagus.

Serves 4.

Fish with Tartar Sauce

INGREDIENTS:
500 g of fish (perch, salmon, etc.)
1 egg beaten
breadcrumbs
salt
pepper

vegetable oil
Tartar sauce (see recipe)

INSTRUCTIONS:
Cut the fish into serving pieces. Dip the pieces in beaten egg. Roll in breadcrumbs. Fry in vegetable oil 5-7 minutes on every side until readiness.
Remove to plate. Put Tartar sauce on top of each fish piece.

Serves 3.

Fresh Herb Marinated Rack Of Lamb With Vinaigrette

INGREDIENTS:
4 racks This recipe is good for 4 of lamb, or 32 ribs.

For the Lamb:
1/4 cup fresh mint chopped
1/4 cup fresh basil chopped
1/4 cup green onions chopped
2 tablespoons fresh oregano chopped
2 tablespoons balsamic vinegar
3 tablespoons olive oil
4 racks of lamb

For vinaigrette:
1 cup olive oil
3/4 cup fresh chopped mint
3/4 cup fresh chopped basil
10 tablespoons red wine vinegar
2 tablespoons fresh chopped oregano
4 tablespoons Dijon mustard
2 teaspoons sugar
1 teaspoon salt
1 cup chopped tomatoes

INSTRUCTIONS:
For the lamb:
In a small bowl, combine mint, basil, green onions, oregano, balsamic vinegar, olive oil.

Line a baking dish with aluminum foil. Generously rub mixture all over the lamb. Cover and chill overnight.

Preheat oven to 375°F. In a large skillet, heat 2 tablespoons olive oil. In batches, sear lamb and place back in the baking dish. Cook for approximately 15-20 minutes, or until an instant read thermometer reaches 145°F.

Remove from the oven and place on a cutting board. Tent with foil. Slice and serve with vinaigrette.

For the vinaigrette:
In a small bowl, combine all ingredients, cover and store in the refrigerator overnight. Bring to room temperature before serving

Serves 12.

Source: "Foodista.com – The Cooking Encyclopedia Everyone Can Edit".

Garlic and Rosemary Roasted Lamb Leg

INGREDIENTS:
1 (6-pound) boneless leg of lamb, trimmed and tied
12 large garlic cloves, unpeeled and divided
1 tablespoon chopped fresh rosemary leaves
salt
2 tablespoons unsalted butter, melted
4 1/2 pounds small red potatoes, unpeeled
2 tablespoons extra virgin olive oil

INSTRUCTIONS:
Preheat the oven to 450°F. Place the oven rack in the lower third of the oven so the lamb will sit in the middle of the oven.

Peel 6 of the cloves of garlic and place them in the bowl of a food processor fitted with the steel blade. Add the rosemary, 1 tablespoon salt, 1 teaspoon pepper, and butter. Process until the garlic and rosemary are finely minced. Thoroughly coat the top and sides of the lamb with the rosemary mixture. Allow to sit at room temperature for 30 minutes to 1 hour.

Toss the potatoes and remaining unpeeled garlic in a bowl with the olive oil and sprinkle with salt. Place in the bottom of a large roasting pan. Place the lamb on top of the potatoes and roast for 1 1/4 to 1 1/2 hours, or until the internal temperature of the lamb is 135°F (rare) or 145°F (medium).

Remove from the oven and put the lamb on a platter; cover tightly with aluminum foil. Allow the lamb to rest for about 20 minutes.

Slice and serve with the potatoes.

Source: "Foodista.com – The Cooking Encyclopedia Everyone Can Edit".

Green Eggs and Ham

INGREDIENTS:
1/8 cup French green lentils
1 thick slice ham
1 egg

INSTRUCTIONS:
Butter a small (6 oz) ramekin.

Add lentils. Spread evenly on bottom.

Add 1 thick slice ham cut to cover the lentils.

Crack the large fresh egg over ham and lentils.

Place ramekin(s) on a cookie sheet.

Bake at 350°F approximately 15 minutes or until egg is cooked: egg white is firm, egg yolk is still soft.

Source: "Foodista.com – The Cooking Encyclopedia Everyone Can Edit".

Heavenly Artichoke Risotto

INGREDIENTS:
4 tablespoons olive oil
1 onion, chopped
1 garlic clove
8 fresh artichoke
5 cups or so fresh vegetable stock
3/4 cup dry white wine
cup scant 2 risotto rice - Arborio or Carnaroli are best
salt
pepper
Parmesan cheese

INSTRUCTIONS:
Start by cleaning your artichokes and soaking them in lemon water.

Heat the oil in a pan, add the onion and garlic and cook for 10 minutes or so over med-low heat without browning.

Chop up the artichokes and saute them slowly until tender - so you could mush with a fork.

Add a couple of spoonfuls of vegetable stock to help the process along and keep from browning the 'chokes.

Now raise the heat, add the rice and saute for a minute or two. Add in the wine and let it cook a little.

Season with salt and pepper.

Meanwhile, bring the stock to a boil in another pan.

Add a ladle-full of the hot stock and cook, stirring, until it has been absorbed into the rice.

Continue adding the stock, a ladle-full at a time, constantly stirring until each addition has been absorbed. This will take 18-20 minutes.

When the rice is firm but not hard (al'dente), turn off the heat, add in a handful or two of graded cheese and give the rice one more stir, check seasoning. Rice should be thick and creamy but not runny. Cover the pot and allow the rice to sit for a couple of minutes.

To serve, spoon the rice into the bowls and sprinkle with parmesan, drizzle with extra virgin olive oil and serve immediately.

Buy a couple of extra chokes' and You can top the dish with a couple of the hearts steamed or boiled separately.

Serve immediately.

Serves 6.

Source: "Foodista.com – The Cooking Encyclopedia Everyone Can Edit".

Herb and Salt Crusted Standing Rib Roast

INGREDIENTS:
7 pounds 3-bone standing beef roast, cut from the loin end, chine bone and fat cap remove
2 cups salt
1 large egg white
3 tablespoons Freshly ground black pepper
3 tablespoons fresh chopped thyme, stems included
2 tablespoons chopped juniper berries
2 tablespoons chopped fresh flat-leaf parsley
2 1/2 cups unbleached all-purpose flour (plus more for rolling)

INSTRUCTIONS:
In a stand mixer fitted with the paddle attachment, combine 1 cup water with the salt, egg white, pepper, thyme, juniper, garlic, and parsley. Mix on medium speed until blended. On medium-low speed, mix in 2 cups of the flour, adding more as needed, until the dough is firm and feels slightly dry and stiff, like Play-Doh. Continue to mix for 2 minutes. The dough should be smooth and firm but not sticky; add more flour if

necessary. Flatten the dough into a rectangle, wrap in plastic, and refrigerate for at least 2 hours and up to 6 hours.

An hour before you are ready to roast, put the beef on the counter and let sit at room temperature.

Place a rack in the center of the oven and heat the oven to 350°F. Heat a large cast-iron skillet over medium-high heat. Add oil and put the roast meat side down in the skillet; sear until deeply browned, about 5 minutes. Remove the roast from the pan and set it bone side down on a rack in a roasting pan.

On a lightly floured surface, roll the dough into a 1/4-inch thick rectangle. Drape the dough over the meat, tucking it in at all sides. Roast until an instant thermometer in the middle of the roast registers 125°F for rare or 135°F for medium-rare, 1 3/4 to 2 1/4 hours. Let rest for 20 minutes, then remove and discard crust.

Carve and serve.

Serves 4.

Source: "Foodista.com – The Cooking Encyclopedia Everyone Can Edit".

Herbed Leg of Lamb

INGREDIENTS:
2 (8 pound) legs of lamb
1 tablespoon cooking spray
4 teaspoon salt
3/4 teaspoon ground pepper
3/4 teaspoon wet rosemary leaves

INSTRUCTIONS:
Put the lamb leg, thin side up, in a deep roasting sheet. Brush cooking spray over the lamb.

Combine salt, ground pepper, and wet rosemary leaves. Mix well. Smear the leg with the mix. Cook the lamb at a 390°F for about 3 hours. Let stand awhile before carving and serving.

Honey Roasted Ham

INGREDIENTS:
5 pounds Ham, boneless
2 cups Honey
1/2 cup Cider vinegar
2 teaspoons Ground cloves
2 cups Brown sugar, packed
2 teaspoons Ground cinnamon

INSTRUCTIONS:
Combine honey, vinegar, cloves, sugar, and cinnamon until well combined. Cook over low heat until sauce almost reaches the boiling point. Remove from heat.

Slice ham halfway through into desired thickness for servings. Tie with string and place in a roasting pan.

Pour sauce over ham, cover and marinate in the refrigerator for 24 hours.

Two hours prior to baking, remove ham from refrigerator and bring to room temperature. Bake at 275°F for about 1 hour, basting occasionally, to heat through. Glaze top under broiler if desired. Carefully monitor while under broiler so as not to burn.

Serves 8.

Source: "Foodista.com – The Cooking Encyclopedia Everyone Can Edit".

Mint-Roasted Lamb Leg

Leg of lamb is a traditional main course for Easter.

INGREDIENTS:
1 (7- to 9-pound) leg of lamb
12 garlic cloves
12 fresh mint leaves
1 teaspoon salt
1/2 teaspoon black pepper
1/4 cup (1/2 stick) butter, melted

INSTRUCTIONS:
Heat oven to 330°F. Lay a roasting pan with aluminum foil and sprinkle the foil with cooking spray.

Using knife, pierce the surface of lamb evenly a number of times (say 20), making each slit about 1 1/2 inches deep. Push garlic cloves in some slits and mint leaves in others. Rub lamb with salt and black pepper and place in roasting pan. Brush with melted butter.

Roast basting with pan juices every 30 minutes for 3 - 3 1/2 hours, or until the meat thermometer registers 160°F - for medium, or until desired doneness beyond that.

Serves 6.

Pink Salmon Baked with Cheese

INGREDIENTS:
500 g pink salmon
150 g cheese grated
mayonnaise
salt
pepper

INSTRUCTIONS:
Cut the fish into serving pieces. Put in baking dish. Salt and pepper. Spread mayonnaise. Sprinkle with cheese.

Place in a preheated oven at 355°F (180°C) for about 1/2 hours until golden crust.

Serves 3.

Pork Baked in Foil with Garlic

INGREDIENTS:
700 g pork filet
5-6 garlic cloves
mustard
salt
black pepper

INSTRUCTIONS:
Cut every garlic clove into 2-4 pieces. Using knife, pierce the surface of pork evenly a number of times. Push garlic pieces in the slits. Rub the meat with salt and black pepper. Spread mustard on the pork. Wrap the pork with foil and place in a preheated oven at 355°F (180°C) for about 1 1/2 hours.

Garnish with mashed potatoes or cooked rice.

Serves 7-8.

Pork Fried with Cheese

INGREDIENTS:
500-700 g filet pork
2 eggs
100 g Parmesan grated
100 g breadcrumbs
salt
pepper
vegetable oil

INSTRUCTIONS:
Cut pork into 1-cm thick pieces. Beat eggs with salt and pepper. Mix parmesan and breadcrumbs.

Dip pieces of pork in beaten eggs. Roll in cheese-breadcrumbs mixture. Fry on every side 7-8 minutes until readiness.

Red Wine Braised Beef Brisket

INGREDIENTS:
4 large garlic cloves, smashed
1/2 teaspoon salt, plus more for seasoning
4 sprigs fresh rosemary, needles striped from the stem and chopped
1/4 cup extra-virgin olive oil
1 (4 pound) beef brisket
Freshly ground black pepper
4 large carrots, cut into chunks
3 celery stalks, cut into chunks
4 large red onions, halved
2 cups dry red wine
1 can (16 ounces) whole tomatoes, hand-crushed
1 handful fresh flat-leaf parsley leaves
3 bay leaves
1 tablespoon all-purpose flour (optional)

INSTRUCTIONS:
Preheat the oven to 325 degrees F.

On a cutting board, mash the garlic and 1/2 teaspoon of the salt together into a paste. Add the rosemary and continue to mash until incorporated. Put the garlic-rosemary paste in a small bowl and add 2 tablespoons of olive oil; stir to combine.

Season both sides of the brisket with a fair amount of kosher salt and ground black pepper. Place a large roasting pan or Dutch oven over medium-high flame and coat with the remaining olive oil. Put the brisket in the roasting pan and sear to form a nice brown crust on both sides. Lay the vegetables all around the brisket and pour the rosemary paste over the whole thing. Add the wine and tomatoes; toss in the parsley and bay leaves. Cover the pan tightly with aluminum foil and transfer to the oven. Bake for about 3 to 4 hours, basting every 30 minutes with the pan juices, until the beef is fork tender.

Remove the brisket to a cutting board and let it rest for 15 minutes. Scoop the vegetables out of the roasting pan and onto a platter, cover to keep warm. Pour out some of the excess fat, and put the roasting pan with the pan juices on the stove over medium-high heat. Boil and stir for 5 minutes until the sauce is reduced by 1/2. (If you want a thicker sauce, mix 1 tablespoon of flour with 2 tablespoons of wine or water and blend into the gravy).

Slice the brisket across the grain (the muscle lines) at a slight diagonal.

Source: "Foodista.com – The Cooking Encyclopedia Everyone Can Edit".

Roasted Asparagus

INGREDIENTS:
2 pounds asparagus spears, tough ends removed
5 garlic cloves, crushed
1 teaspoon olive oil
1/2 teaspoon sea salt
3 tablespoons balsamic vinegar

INSTRUCTIONS:
Line a baking sheet with foil or parchment paper. Lay the asparagus on the sheet in a single layer. Toss garlic, olive oil, and salt. Roast in a 425°F degree F (220°C) oven (no need to preheat the oven) for 15 minutes or until just tender when pierced with a knife. Before serving, toss with balsamic vinegar.

Salmon Baked with Cheese

INGREDIENTS:
500 g salmon
150 g cheese grated
mayonnaise
salt
pepper

INSTRUCTIONS:
Cut the fish into serving pieces. Put in baking dish. Salt and pepper. Spread mayonnaise. Sprinkle with cheese.

Place in a preheated oven at 355°F (180°C) for about 1/2 hours until golden crust.

Serves 3.

Salmon with Sorrel Sauce

INGREDIENTS:
300 g salmon
1 egg
Flour
vegetable oil
salt

For Sorrel Sauce:
50 g sorrel finely chopped
100 g onions minced
200 ml cream (20-30%)
1 tablespoon flour
water
salt

INSTRUCTIONS:
Prepare sauce:
In saucepan fry onions in vegetable oil until golden. Add sorrel and 2-3 tablespoon water. Simmer for 2-3 minutes. Add cream and mix well. Add flour, a little salt and mix well. Bring to a boil, but do not boil. Put the sauce in a blender and mix well.

Prepare Salmon:
Dip the fish in flour. Dip in beaten egg with salt. Dip again in flour. Fry in vegetable oil until golden brown on both sides. Remove to plate. Serve with Sorrel sauce on top of each fish piece.

Sausage Scalloped Potatoes

INGREDIENTS:
6 medium potatoes
1 cup American cheese
1/2 pound smoked sausage
1 cup Milk
Salt and pepper

INSTRUCTIONS:
Peel and slice potatoes thin. Slice sausage thin. Layer potatoes and sausage in a 2-quart casserole with cheese. Cover with milk and season with salt and pepper. Bake in oven until potatoes are done. Bake at 350°F.

Serves 2.

Source: "Foodista.com – The Cooking Encyclopedia Everyone Can Edit".

Sweet and Spicy Shrimp

INGREDIENTS:
2 pounds Shrimp, large 25-31 count, peeled and deveined
1 tablespoon Cajun Spice blend
2 teaspoons Olive oil
1 cup Orange juice
1/2 cup Apricot preserves
4 cups Hot cooked rice
3 Each Green onions, chopped

INSTRUCTIONS:
Combine the cleaned shrimp with the Cajun spice blend and reserve.

Combine the orange juice and apricot preserves in a small saucepan and heat until the preserves are melted into the orange juice, continue to simmer until slightly thickened.

Heat the olive oil in a very hot saute pan over high heat and add the shrimp. Saute the shrimp evenly on all sides until almost pink, then add the orange juice mixture to the shrimp. Heat through until the shrimp are pink, but not over cooked.

Serve each portion with 1/2 cup of cooked rice and 3/4 cup of the shrimp and sauce. Garnish with the green onions.

Serves 8.

Source: "Foodista.com – The Cooking Encyclopedia Everyone Can Edit".

Desserts, Baking

Ambrosia or Fruit Salad For Dessert

INGREDIENTS:
1/2 cup shredded coconut
1 small can mandarin oranges, drained
1/2 cup pineapple chunks, drained
1 cup miniature marshmallows
1/2 cup sour cream with 1 tablespoon mayonnaise
1 drop of lemon juice

INSTRUCTIONS:
Mix slowly all ingredients together. Let stand in refrigerator 24 hours. Garnish with chopped nuts, maraschino cherries (color green and red for Holidays). Use pastel colored marshmallows for Easter.

Serves 6.

Source: "Foodista.com – The Cooking Encyclopedia Everyone Can Edit".

Babka

Ukrainian bread also made at Easter.

INGREDIENTS:
2 cups unsifted flour
1/4 cup sugar
1 pkg. Fleischmann's active dry yeast
1/4 cup butter
3 eggs, room temperature
1/4 cup seedless raisins
1/2 cup milk

INSTRUCTIONS:
In a large bowl, thoroughly mix 3/4 cup flour, sugar, and undissolved yeast.

Combine milk and butter in a saucepan. Heat over low heat until the liquid is warm (butter does not need to melt).

Gradually add to dry ingredients and beat 2 minutes at medium speed of electric mixer, scraping bowl occasionally.

Add eggs and 1/2 cup flour or enough flour to make a thick batter. Beat at high speed 2 minutes, scraping bowl occasionally.

Add the remaining flour and beat 2 minutes at high speed. Cover; let rise in a warm place, free from draft, until bubbly (about 1 hour).

Stir in raisins; turn in a greased and floured 2 quart tube pan. Let rise, uncovered, in a warm place (free from draft) for 30 minutes.

Bake in moderate heat in the oven (350°F) for about 40 minutes or until done.

Makes 1 loaf.

Source: "Foodista.com – The Cooking Encyclopedia Everyone Can Edit".

Baby Chick Cupcakes

INGREDIENTS:
2 1/4 cups plain flour
1 1/4 cups sugar
1 cup butter
1 cup milk
2 1/2 teaspoons baking powder
1 teaspoon salt
1 teaspoon vanilla
1 egg
2 cups icing sugar
cream
yellow food colouring
2 cups coconut
Brown and orange M&Ms

INSTRUCTIONS:
Heat oven to 180°C (355°F). Put paper cases in 24 muffin tins (or halve
the recipe and do 12, or bake 12 at a time).

In a medium bowl, beat flour, sugar, butter, milk, baking powder, salt,
vanilla and egg. Either beat 3 minutes with a mixer, or get that baking
bicep out and mix by hand for a few minutes. Fill paper cases half full.

Bake 15-20 minutes until a toothpick inserted in the centre comes out
clean. Cool completely on a rack.

FROSTING:
This is the fun part! Add tablespoonful of cream to the two cups of icing
in a bowl, until it gets to the desired stage. Some people like it runny.

Add a few drops of yellow food coloring and mix.

Now for the chick feathers... add 2 cups coconut to a ziplock bag, drop in
some food coloring, seal it up and rub it all with your fingers to dye the
coconut.

When cupcakes are completely cool, ice with yellow frosting. Put the
coconut in a small bowl, and dip the cupcakes icing-side down into it to

completely cover. Add brown M&Ms for eyes, sticking on with a little frosting for glue. Poke orange M&Ms in for the beak...

Source: "Foodista.com – The Cooking Encyclopedia Everyone Can Edit".

Braided Easter Bread

INGREDIENTS:
2 1/4 to 3 1/4 cups flour
1/4 cup sugar
1 teaspoon salt
1 package rapid-rise dry yeast
2 eggs, beaten
2/3 cup warm milk
2 tablespoons butter, melted
1 tablespoon anise seed
1/2 cup candied fruit (optional)
1/4 cup chopped nuts (optional)
5 raw colored eggs

INSTRUCTIONS:
In a bowl, mix 1 cup of the flour, sugar, salt, and yeast. Pour in a saucepan milk. Add dry mixture from the bowl,
melted butter mixture and eggs. Whisk the mixture for 2 minutes. To make a soft dough stir in enough of the remaining flour, anise seed and any of the candied fruit or nuts. Knead for 8 to 10 minutes. The dough should not be sticky so add flour as necessary. Let the batter rise for about 1– 1 1/2 hour or until double in size.

Divide dough in two pieces. Roll each of them into 24-inch rope. Twist 2 pieces together connecting the 4 end pieces so the dough forms a wreath. Place the wreath on a greased baking sheet. Place the five colored eggs into spaces between twists. Brush the wreath with melted butter. Let the dough rise for 1 hour. Bake at 350°F for 35–50 minutes.

Braided Easter Bread With Eggs

INGREDIENTS:

1 package active dry yeast
1/2 cup lukewarm water
2 cups to 2 1/2 flour
3/4 stick butter, softened
1/2 cup sugar
Juice and grated rind of 1 lemon
1/4 teaspoon salt
1 egg
4 whole uncooked eggs, plain or colored for Easter

INSTRUCTIONS:
In a small bowl, dissolve yeast in 1/4 cup of lukewarm water. Set aside.

In a medium mixing bowl, add remaining water and 1 cup flour. Using an electric mixer, mix in yeast until well blended and smooth. Cover bowl with plastic wrap and a towel and place in a warm place to rise, 1 to 2 hours. This mixture should double in bulk.

In an electric mixer, cream butter. Gradually add sugar and beat until light. Add lemon juice and rind and salt. Add egg.

Add raised yeast mixture and mix well.

With a wooden spoon, stir in about 1 to 1 1/2 cups of flour. Turn dough out onto a floured surface and knead to form a soft non-sticky dough. Shape into a ball. Place dough in a greased bowl. Cover with plastic wrap and a towel and let rise in a warm place until doubled in bulk, about 2 hours.

Punch down the dough with your fist. Divide the dough into 2 equal pieces. Roll each piece of dough into a long cylinder about 1 1/2 inches thick.

Loosely twist two pieces of dough together to form a loose braid. Form the braid into a ring shape and place on a parchment-lined cookie sheet. Place uncooked eggs into spaces in braid. Cover with plastic wrap and towel and let rise until doubled in a warm spot, about 40 minutes. Remove plastic wrap and towel.

Preheat oven to 375°F.

Bake for 25 to 30 minutes, or until golden brown.

Remove from the oven. Cool bread in a pan on wire rack. Serve warm or cold. When cool, if desired, frost the top of the loaf with confectioners' frosting.

Serves 8.

Source: "Foodista.com – The Cooking Encyclopedia Everyone Can Edit".

Chalka - Polish Easter Bread

INGREDIENTS:
1 cup milk
1/2 cup (1 stick) butter or margarine
1 cup sugar
1/2 teaspoon salt
2 packages active dry yeast
1/4 cup warm water
2 eggs
1 teaspoon vanilla
5 1/2 cups flour
1 cup raisins or dried chopped fruit
1 egg for glazing, beaten

INSTRUCTIONS:
Bring milk to a simmer in a pot. Remove from heat and add butter, sugar and salt. Stir until melted. Set aside to cool (you don't want to add it hot or you'll kill the yeast).

Mix yeast with warm water until dissolved, then add milk mixture, eggs and vanilla to combine. Add 3 cups of flour and beat until smooth. Add raisins and remaining flour. A sticky dough will form. Kneed for about 5 minutes, then set into a bowl. Rub with a little oil and cover with plastic. Set in a warm place to rise for about 1 hour or until doubled.

Punch down the dough and divide in 2. You can braid it or form it into any shape you like. Set onto a parchment lined baking sheet and cover again with plastic wrap. Let rise for about 30 minutes.

Preheat oven to 350°F. Brush tops of bread with beaten egg, then bake for 30 minutes. Cool on wire racks.

You can serve this for breakfast or an evening snack with butter and jam. And don't forget the coffee or tea.

Tips: 1. You can color your bread by dividing the beaten egg into smaller bowls, then using a few drops of food coloring. Paint your bread with the colored egg before baking.

2. You can also use this recipe to make buns or smaller loaves. You could get 4 small loaves out of this recipe and give them as gifts when you go visiting your single friends or couples. People with kids will need a full size loaf.

Yield: 6 servings.

Source: "Foodista.com – The Cooking Encyclopedia Everyone Can Edit".

Chocolate Gateau

INGREDIENTS:
1 cup Butter or margarine, softened
1 cup Sugar
3 Eggs
3 ounces Unsweetened chocolate, melted
1 teaspoon Instant coffee crystals
2 cups Sifted all-purpose flour
1 teaspoon Baking soda
teaspoon Salt
1 cup Whipping cream
Chocolate Butter-cream (see recipe)
Chocolate Glaze (see recipe)
Slivered almonds

INSTRUCTIONS:
Cream butter and sugar in large bowl until fluffy. Beat in eggs 1 at a time, blending well after each addition. Mix in chocolate and coffee crystals. Mix in combined flour, baking soda and salt alternately with cream, beginning and ending with dry ingredients.

Pour batter into 2 greased and floured 8 inch round cake pans; bake at 350°F for 20 minutes, or until cake springs back when touched. Cool in pans 10 minutes; remove from pans and cool.

Make Buttercream and glaze.

Cut cake layers in half horizontally with serrated knife. Place 1 cake layer on the serving plate; spread with a third of the buttercream filling. Repeat with remaining layers and Buttercream. Frost top and side of the cake with glaze; garnish with almonds.

Yield: 10 to 12 servings.

NOTE: Cake can be made 2 days in advance; refrigerate.

Source: "Foodista.com – The Cooking Encyclopedia Everyone Can Edit".

Easter Biscuits

INGREDIENTS:
1/2 cup (1 stick) butter
1/2 cup superfine sugar
1 egg, separated
1 cup flour
1/4 teaspoon ground allspice
1/4 teaspoon ground cloves
1/4 cup currants
2 teaspoons grated orange peel (see NOTE)
1 teaspoon grated lemon peel (see NOTE)
2 tablespoons milk
sugar for sprinkling

INSTRUCTIONS:
1. Heat the oven to 400°F (205°C).

2. Mix the butter and sugar until soft and fluffy. Beat in egg yolk but the egg white preserve for step 3. Add the flour and spices. Mix well. Add the orange, currants, lemon peel and enough milk to form a soft dough.

Transfer the dough onto a floured surface and knead. Roll out to about 1/2-inch thick. Use a drinking glass to cut 2-inch circles. Puncture the circles tops with a fork.

3. Put the dough circles onto two greased baking sheets. Bake for 10 minutes and remove from oven. Lightly beat the egg white and brush the biscuits. Sprinkle them with sugar, and return to oven. Bake for additional 5 minutes until the tops of the biscuits are golden brown. Transfer to wire racks to cool. Store the biscuits in an airtight container.

Makes 30 biscuits

NOTE: Avoid getting the white pith, which is bitter.

Easter Hot Cross Buns

INGREDIENTS:
Dough:
2 eggs plus enough water to get 1 1/3 cups
4 ozs / 1 sticks butter meltedave
4 cups bread flour
3/4 teaspoon ground cinnamon
1/4 teaspoon grated nutmeg
1 1/2 teaspoons salt
2 tablespoons sugar
1 1/2 teaspoons quick active yeast
1 cup dried currants
1/2 tablespoon orange zest

Egg Wash:
1 egg yolk
1 tablespoon cold water

Orange Icing:
1/2 cup icing sugar
1/4 tablespoon orange juice
1 drops orange oil

INSTRUCTIONS:

Plonk dough ingredients in your bread machine in the order they are listed except for the currants and the zest, which are to be added 10 minutes before the final kneading cycle ends.

Use dough/manual cycle. This should include the first rising.

Punch down and remove dough from bread machine pan.

With floured hands, knead a little to remove the air bubbles.

Divide the dough into 16 equal pieces, shape into balls and place on oiled baking tray.

Cover with plastic wrap and let rest for 45 mins - 1 hour or until doubled in size. Brush with egg wash and bake in a 180°C (350°F) oven for 10 - 20 minutes.

Cover the top with aluminum foil after 15 mins into the baking to prevent over-browning.

Cool and pipe orange icing over the top.

PS: It's good toasted too but leave out the icing if you intend to do that.

Yield: 8 servings

Source: "Foodista.com – The Cooking Encyclopedia Everyone Can Edit".

Easter Nests

INGREDIENTS:
1 egg white
75g (3oz) caster sugar
25g (1oz) cornflour, sifted
50g (2oz) dark chocolate (at least 70% cocoa solids), grated
16 mini chocolate eggs

INSTRUCTIONS:
Lay baking paper on a baking tray.

Beat the egg white until stiff. Then slowly whisk in half of the sugar. After that fold in the remaining sugar with the cornflour and chocolate. Transfer the mixture to a piping bag with a large star nozzle and pipe 6 1/2cm (2 1/2 inch) nests onto the baking tray.

Heat up the oven to 285°F (140°C). Put the tray into oven and bake for 45 minutes. Leave to cool, then fill with mini chocolate eggs.

Serves 4.

Easter Truffles

INGREDIENTS:
175 g (6 oz) plain chocolate
1 egg yolk
25 g (1 oz) butter softened
1 teaspoon coffee-flavoured liqueur
1 tablespoon cocoa powder

INSTRUCTIONS:
Place the chocolate in a double boiler above simmering water and melt it, occasionally stirring.

Take away the chocolate from the heat and add butter, egg and liqueur. Stir.

Let the mixture cool for 30-40 minutes until firm. Form small eggs by hand from the chocolate mixture. Dredge the chocolate eggs with cocoa powder.

Easter-Egg Bread

INGREDIENTS:
1 cup Sugar
1 teaspoon Salt
1 packet Active dry yeast
1 cup All-purpose flour
2 tablespoons Butter
1 cup Milk

9 Eggs
2 tablespoons Grated lemon peel
Easter-egg coloring kit
1 teaspoon Water

INSTRUCTIONS:
In the bowl, mix sugar, salt, yeast, and 1 cup flour. Heat the butter and milk until very warm (125°F). With a mixer at low speed, beat the liquid into dry ingredients. At medium speed, beat for 2 minutes. Beat in 2 eggs, 1 egg white, and 3/4 cups flour; beat 2 minutes. Stir in lemon peel and 1 1/4 cups flour.

On the floured surface, knead dough about 5 minutes, working in about 1/2 cup flour; place in greased bowl, turning to grease the top. Cover; let rise in a warm place until doubled, about 1 1/2 hours.

Meanwhile, dye 6 eggs in your favorite colors, following the label directions from an Easter-egg coloring kit, but do not hard-cook eggs; set aside.

Punch down dough; turn onto floured surface; cover for 25 minutes.

Grease a large cookie sheet. Cut dough in half; form each half into a 30-inch long rope. On the cookie sheet, twist the ropes together to form a ring, leaving holes for 5 eggs. Cover; let rise until doubled, about 1 1/2 hours

Preheat the oven to 350°F. Insert raw, colored eggs into holes in twist; place 1 egg in the center. In the cup, beat egg yolk with water; use it to brush dough. Bake for 30 minutes or until golden. Cool on wire rack.

Yields 1 loaf.

Source: "Foodista.com – The Cooking Encyclopedia Everyone Can Edit".

French Easter Cream

INGREDIENTS:
1/3 cup raisins
1 tablespoon granulated gelatine

1/4 cup brandy
1/4 cup gin
2 tablespoons cold water
2 cups cream Maraschino
1/2 cup sugar
3 eggs Yolks
1/8 teaspoon salt
1 teaspoon vanilla

INSTRUCTIONS:
Seed raisins, add brandy, and cook in a double boiler until raisins are
soft. Make a custard of cream, sugar, egg yolks and salt. Remove from
the heat, add gelatin soaked in cold water.
Strain, cool slightly, add flavorings, stir until the mixture thickens, then
add raisins. Mould and chill. Remove from mould, and garnish with
Sauterne Jelly (colored violet), cut in cubes, and fresh violets.

Fruit Trifle

INGREDIENTS:
2 cups milk
1 (4-serving size) package instant vanilla pudding and pie filling
5 cups cake cubes
1 (16-ounce) can sliced or diced peaches, drained and juice reserved
1 (8-ounce) can pineapple chunks or tidbits, drained and juice reserved
1 1/2 cups whipped cream or whipped topping

INSTRUCTIONS:
In a bowl, put together milk and pudding mix. Blend with a wire whisk
1-2 minutes, until thickened and set aside.

In a glass serving bowl, put in layers the cake cubes, half peaches and
half pineapple, then half pudding. Repeat layers and finish with the
remaining pudding. Top with whipped cream. Garnish the top with fresh
or canned fruit, cookie crumbs, or toasted nuts. Cover and refrigerate
until ready to serve.

Greek Trinity Loaf

This traditional Greek Easter bread acquires its name from its shape. According to Greek tradition, the bread is cut when the entire family is seated at the Easter table. Each person receives one thin slice from each of the three loaves.

INGREDIENTS:
3 to 3 1/2 cups all-purpose flour (divided)
1/4 cup granulated sugar
2 packages RapidRise or fast-acting yeast
1 teaspoon anise seed
1 teaspoon salt
1/2 cup water (70 to 80°F)
1/3 cup butter or margarine, cut up
2 whole eggs plus 1 separated egg (divided)
1 cup golden raisins

INSTRUCTIONS:
In a large bowl, combine 1 cup flour, sugar, undissolved yeast, anise seed and salt.

Heat water and butter until very warm (120 to 130°F); stir into dry ingredients. Stir in 2 eggs, 1 egg yolk (reserve egg white) and enough remaining flour to make soft dough.

Knead on lightly floured surface until smooth and elastic, about 5 to 7 minutes. Cover; let rest for 10 minutes.

To shape and bake dough: Remove 1/2 cup dough; reserve. Knead raisins into remaining dough; divide into 3 equal pieces. Form each into a smooth ball; arrange on a greased baking sheet in the shape of a 3-leaf clover.

Divide reserved dough into 4 equal pieces; roll each into a 10-inch rope. Place 2 ropes side by side; twist together, pinching ends to seal.

Repeat with remaining ropes.

Arrange twisted ropes on 3-leaf clover in the form of a cross, tucking ends under. Cover; let rise in warm, draft-free place until doubled in size, about 45 to 60 minutes.

Lightly beat reserved egg white; brush on dough. Meanwhile, preheat oven to 375°F.

Bake bread for 30 to 35 minutes or until done, covering with foil after 10 minutes to prevent excess browning.

Remove from pan; cool on wire rack.

Bread machine method: (For 1 1/2- or 2-pound bread machines.) Using 3 1/4 cups bread flour and 3 teaspoons rapid-rise or fast-acting yeast, add ingredients to bread machine pan in the order suggested by manufacturer. Process on dough/manual cycle.

When the cycle is complete, remove the dough to floured surface. If necessary, knead in additional flour to make the dough easy to handle. Proceed as directed above to shape and bake the dough.

Makes 1 loaf.

Honey-Fig Jam

INGREDIENTS:
8 cups figs
4 cups honey
1 lemon finely sliced and chopped

INSTRUCTIONS:
Puree the figs. Add honey and lemon, including rinds. Cook, stirring constantly, until thick. With spoon place the jam into hot sterilized jars to within 1/4 inch from top. Seal the jars. Process in a boiling-water bath for 10 minutes.

Italian Easter Bread

INGREDIENTS:
1 packet cake yeast
1 tablespoon vegetable oil
1 dozen large eggs
juice of 1 lemon
1 pinch salt
1 1/2 cups sugar
1 ounce anisette
3 1/2 pounds (14 cups) flour
1/2 cup powdered sugar
2 tablespoons milk
1 teaspoon vanilla extract
10 smalls colored eggs (optional)
1/2 cup candied citron, chopped (optional)
colored candies (optional)

INSTRUCTIONS:
Dissolve yeast in a little warm water. Add oil and set aside.

In a large bowl, combine eggs, lemon juice, salt, sugar, anisette, and citron if desired. Mix with your hands.

Add in yeast mixture and flour. Knead well.

Set in a warm place. Let rise till double - about 1 hour.

Punch down, let rise another hour.

Shape into two large loaves, or to create a traditional braided Easter Bread, separate the dough into four equal parts. Roll each part to about 36 inches long and 1 1/2 inches thick.

Using two long pieces of dough, form a loosely braided ring, leaving spaces for five colored (uncooked) eggs. Seal the ends of the ring together and use your fingers to slide the eggs between the braids of dough.

Repeat with remaining rolled dough.

Bake at 350°F until brown (less than 1 hour).

While still warm, glaze with thin icing of powdered sugar, vanilla, and milk. Add colored candies, if desired.

Yield: 2 large loaves.

Source: "Foodista.com – The Cooking Encyclopedia Everyone Can Edit".

Italian Nougat

This candy is usually made only during the Easter holidays.

INGREDIENTS:
1 cup Blanched Hazelnuts
2 (4 1/2 oz) package blanched Whole almonds
2 cups Table sugar
1 cup Light corn syrup
1/2 cup Fresh honey
1/4 teaspoon salt
2 egg whites
2 teaspoons vanilla extract
1/4 cup Butter or margarine softened

INSTRUCTIONS:
1. Preheat oven to 350°F. Spread hazelnuts and almonds on cookie sheet. Toast in oven 10 minutes, until golden.

2. In heavy, straight-side, 3-quart saucepan, combine sugar, corn syrup, honey, salt, and 1/4 cup water. Stir over medium heat, until sugar is dissolved. Continue cooking, without stirring, to 252°F, on candy thermometer, or until a small amount in cold water forms a hard ball.

3. Meanwhile, beat egg whites at high speed, in a large bowl of electric mixer, until forming stiff peaks.

4. In a thin stream, pour about 1/4 of hot syrup over egg whites, beating constantly, at high speed, 5 minutes until the mixture is stiff enough to hold its shape. Cook the rest of the syrup to 315-318°F on candy thermometer, or until a small amount in cold water forms brittle threads.

5. In a thin stream, pour hot syrup over meringue, beating constantly, at high speed, until stiff enough to hold its shape.

6. Add vanilla and butter, beating until thickened, again-about 5 minutes. With wooden spoon stir in toasted nuts.

7. Turn mixture onto a buttered 11x7x1-1/4 inch pan. Smooth the top with a spatula. Refrigerate until firm.

8. Loosen the edge of the candy all around; turn out in a large block. With a sharp knife, cut into 1-1/2x1-inch pieces.

9. Wrap each in waxed paper.

10. Refrigerate.

Source: "Foodista.com – The Cooking Encyclopedia Everyone Can Edit".

Kid Cupcakes

INGREDIENTS:
1 (18 1/2 oz.) package white cake mix with 26 flat-bottomed "cake cup" ice cream cones
1 can commercial cream cheese frosting
Flaked coconut, chocolate morsels, red hots,

INSTRUCTIONS:
Prepare cake mix according to package. Spoon 1/4 batter into each cone and place cones in muffin pans. Bake at 350°F for 20 to 25 minutes. Cool on wire rack. Spread with frosting and decorate according to the occasion. For Easter, make jelly bean faces, or a Santa face for Christmas.

Source: "Foodista.com – The Cooking Encyclopedia Everyone Can Edit".

Kulich

Easter bread, traditional in the Orthodox Christian faith and eaten in Russia, Belarus, Bulgaria and Serbia.

INGREDIENTS:
2 package rapid rise yeast
1 tablespoon vanilla
1 tablespoon grated orange peel
1 tablespoon grated lemon peel
1 teaspoon lemon juice freshly squeezed
9 eggs
12 cups flour approximately
3 cups golden or dark raisins or both
1 cup chopped walnuts or pecans
3/4 cup lukewarm water
4 cups undiluted evaporated milk
1 cup sugar
4 cups flour
1 tablespoon ground cardamom
1 1/2 cups butter
3 cups sugar
2 tablespoons salt

INSTRUCTIONS:
In a small saucepan, scald the milk. Do this by bringing the temperature to a high simmer quickly (bubbles will begin to form along the edge). Turn off and remove from heat. Allow to cool to lukewarm. A skin will form. (If no skin forms, the milk wasn't heated sufficiently).

Skim the skin from the top. This removes a protein which is not beneficial to the bread making process.

Dissolve yeast in water which is lukewarm. Set aside.

In a mixing bowl, add the dissolved yeast and 1 cup of sugar to the cooled milk with 3-4 cups flour along with the cardamom. Stir together, cover, and set this (the sponge) in a warm place, free from draft to rise for several hours.

When the sponge has risen to about double in bulk, melt the butter in a small saucepan. Stir in lemon and orange zest, 3 cups sugar, vanilla, and salt. Allow to cool to lukewarm and stir this mixture into the sponge. Add the lemon juice.

Begin to stir in the flour, a 1/2 cup at a time until the dough can be turned out onto a floured board to be kneaded. Knead the dough until it becomes smooth and elastic (5-10 minutes), adding in additional flour as needed to prevent the dough from sticking. However, do not add too much flour or the finished bread will be heavy.

Knead in the raisins and nuts. Knead an additional 5 minutes, and place dough in a large bowl greased with butter or oil, turning once to grease the top. Cover and place in a warm place, free from draft, to rise until nearly doubled in bulk. This may take several hours.

After the dough has risen, roll into balls of different sizes and place into greased coffee tins or bread pans. Or you may braid the dough and place on a cookie sheet.

Brush the top with an egg wash* and bake in a preheated 350 degree oven until bread is golden brown on top and tapping the bottom of the loaf sounds hollow. With experience, you'll be able to tell when the bread is done because the house will smell like a bakery! *Egg wash: Mix the white of an egg with a tablespoon of water. This imparts a glossy sheen to the top of the bread and also allows you to adhere poppy seeds or sesame seeds to the top

Remove bread from pans and set on a wire rack to cool. Don't set it directly on a dish or the bottom will steam. Brush the tops with butter and allow to cool before slicing with a serrated knife.

Source: "Foodista.com – The Cooking Encyclopedia Everyone Can Edit".

Limoncello Tiramisu

INGREDIENTS:
5 large eggs
5 lemons
1 cup sugar
1 1/2 cups limoncello liqueur
1 cup water

1 pound (2 cups) Mascarpone, at room temperature
40 ladyfingers (preferably imported Italian savoiardi), or more as needed

INSTRUCTIONS:
Pour just enough water in the double-boiler pan so the water level is right below the bottom of the mixing bowl when it is sitting in the pan. Separate the eggs, putting yolks into the large bowl of the double boiler and the whites into another stainless-steel bowl for whipping by hand or with an electric mixer.

Remove the zest of two or more of the lemons, using a fine grater, to get 2 tablespoons of zest. Squeeze out and strain the juice of these and the other lemons to get 3/4 cup of fresh lemon juice.

To make the base for the tiramisù, heat the water in the double boiler to a steady simmer. Off the heat, beat the egg yolks with 1/4 cup of the sugar and 1/2 cup of the limoncello until well blended. Set the bowl over the simmering water, and whisk constantly, frequently scraping the whisk around the sides and bottom of the bowl, as the egg mixture expands and heats into a frothy sponge, 5 minutes or longer. When the sponge has thickened enough to form a ribbon when it drops on the surface, take the bowl off the double-boiler pan and let it cool.

Meanwhile, pour the remaining cup of limoncello, all of the lemon juice, 1 cup water, and 1/2 cup of the sugar in a saucepan. Bring to a boil, stirring to dissolve the sugar, and cook for 5 minutes, evaporating the alcohol. Let the syrup cool completely.

In another large bowl, stir the mascarpone with a wooden spoon to soften it, then drop in the grated lemon zest and beat until light and creamy. Whip the egg whites with the remaining 1/4 cup sugar, by hand or by machine, until it holds moderately firm peaks.

When the cooked limoncello sponge (or zabaglione) is cooled, scrape about a third of it over the mascarpone, and fold it in with a large rubber spatula. Fold in the rest of the zabaglione in two or three additions. Now fold in the whipped egg whites in several additions, until the limoncello-mascarpone cream is light and evenly blended.

Pour some of the cooled syrup, no deeper than 1/4 inch, into the shallow-rimmed pan to moisten the ladyfingers (savoiardi). One at a time, roll a ladyfinger in the syrup and place it in the casserole or baking dish. Wet each cookie briefly - if it soaks up too much syrup, it will fall apart. Arrange the moistened ladyfingers in neat, tight rows, filling the bottom of the pan completely. You should be able to fit about twenty ladyfingers in a single layer.

Scoop half of the limoncello-mascarpone cream onto the ladyfingers, and smooth it to fill the pan and cover them. Dip and arrange a second layer of ladyfingers in the pan, and cover it completely with the remainder of the cream.

Smooth the cream with the spatula, and seal the tiramisu airtight in a plastic wrap. Before serving, refrigerate for 6 hours (or up to 2 days), or put it in the freezer for 2 hours. To serve, cut portions of tiramisu in any size you like, and serve each out of the pan and onto dessert plates.

Serves 12.
Source: "Foodista.com - the Cooking Encyclopedia Everyone Can Edit".

Penuche Fudge

INGREDIENTS:
1 cup Brown Sugar (light, packed)
1 1/2 cups Granulated Sugar
1 cup Light Cream (or Half-and-Half)
1 cup Milk
2 tablespoons Butter
1/2 cup Pecans (preferred) or Walnuts (chopped)
1 teaspoon Vanilla Extract

INSTRUCTIONS:
Combine sugars, milk, and cream in a 2-quart sauce pan and bring to medium heat until sugars dissolved. Bring to a rolling boil stirring constantly until candy thermometer reaches 236°F (soft-ball drop stage) or for about 8 minutes. Remove from heat and add butter stirring until melted. Let set unstirred until the temperature is 110°F (uncomfortable to touch but won't burn you) then add vanilla and stir vigorously (5-10 minutes) until the mixture cools enough to lose its glossy texture. Fold in nuts and pour.

Portuguese Easter Bread

INGREDIENTS:
4 cups milk
1 teaspoon salt
1/2 pound lard
Three 1/4-ounce envelopes active dry yeast
5 pounds flour (St. Elizabeth or Rose brand preferred)
12 large eggs
4 cups sugar
Zest of 1 lemon, grated
1 large egg beaten with 1 tablespoon water, for glaze
5 uncooked eggs for top of each bread (optional)

INSTRUCTIONS:
1. Combine in a saucepan the milk, salt and lard. Mix well and bring to boil. Put aside.

2. Combine in another bowl the yeast, 1 cup flour, and 1/2 cup warm water. Mix well and also put aside.

3. Put in a third bowl the eggs, sugar and lemon zest. Mix well. Add the milk mixture from the first bowl. Add yeast mixture from the second bowl. Also add remaining flour. Mix well. Set apart to rise for 6 hours. During this period knead 5 times every half hour. Divide the batter to 5 equal pieces.

4. Grease a round loaf pan with lard. Put 1 piece of dough in the pan. The pan should be half-full. Let the batter to rise until it reaches the top of the pan (if you choose to add the 5 eggs for Easter, then place one egg on top of the dough). Then brush the dough piece with beaten egg and bake it for about 1 hour in the oven at a temperature of 350°F, until golden brown. Remove the bread to a wire racks and cool before serving.

5. Repeat the step 4 with each piece of batter or use 5 pans to bake the bread.

Yield: 5 loafs (8 to 10 servings).

Ricotta Pie

INGREDIENTS:
9 inches pie crust
2 eggs
2 teaspoons vanilla extract
1/2 cup Sugar
1 teaspoon ground cinnamon
1/8 teaspoon Orange Extract
extra cinnamon to sprinkle on top

INSTRUCTIONS:
Preheat oven at 350°F.

In a large bowl mix all ingredients until ricotta mixture is smooth.

Pour ricotta mixture on pie crust, sprinkle the top lightly with cinnamon and bake for about 1 hour or until ready, i.e. when the knife in the center comes out clean.

When ready, switch pie on bottom rack and bake for another 10 minutes so the bottom of the crust is cooked. Remove from oven and refrigerate for at least 2 hours before serving.

Source: "Foodista.com – The Cooking Encyclopedia Everyone Can Edit".

Rohrnudeln

INGREDIENTS:
2 1/2 cups flour, plus 1/4 cup flour (if needed)
1/4 cup sugar
2 large eggs, room temperature
3/4 cup milk
4 tablespoons unsalted butter
1 package rapid rise yeast
8 tablespoons apricot preserves (or your choice)

For the bottom of the baking pan:
3 tablespoons butter
1/4 cup sugar melted (to dip unbaked rolls into)

INSTRUCTIONS:
Preheat Oven to 350°F. Spray a glass square baking dish with non-stick cooking spray, or line with parchment paper.

Mix dry ingredients, and add yeast.

Add warm milk and butter to dry ingredients, mix.

Allow to rise (about 45 minutes); then gently knead.

Divide dough in half, then fourths; shape and add preserves in the middle.

Melt some butter and sugar; dip each roll into this and put into a baking pan.

Bake at 350°F 30 minutes or until golden.

Yield 9 rolls.

Source: "Foodista.com – The Cooking Encyclopedia Everyone Can Edit".

Strawberries and Cream Layers Cake

INGREDIENTS:
1 (18 1/2-ounce) package white cake mix
2 (10-ounce) packages frozen strawberries, thawed and pureed
1 (12-ounce) container frozen whipped topping, thawed
1 cup fresh strawberries, cleaned, hulled, and sliced

INSTRUCTIONS:
Warm oven and make cake mix in accordance to the package directions. Bake the dough in two 9-inch round baking pans. Cool the cakes and

when they are cooled completely, cut each of them horizontally in two. So you make 4 layers.

Put one layer on a large serving plate. Brush with pureed strawberries and spread with whipped topping. Put another cake layer over the first, brush with pureed strawberries and spread with the topping. Repeat until all cake layers, strawberries, and whipped topping are used.

Garnish with fresh strawberry slices and serve immediately, or cover the cake lightly and keep chilled until you will be ready to serve.

Swedish Easter Bread

INGREDIENTS:
1 cup milk
1/2 stick butter
1 pkg. dry yeast
1/4 cup warm water
1/2 cup sugar
1/2 teaspoon salt
3 cups flour
1 egg
12 cardamom pods

INSTRUCTIONS:
Scald milk. Add butter to melt. Cool to lukewarm. Dissolve yeast in 1/4 cup warm water. Add remaining ingredients. Add enough flour to be able to handle dough for kneading. Knead about 3 to 4 minutes. Cover with saran wrap in a large bowl and allow to rise 2 to 3 hours.

Remove dough, divide into 2 pieces for 2 loaves. Take each half and divide into 3 sections and roll into strips. Now these 3 strips can be braided. Repeat with another half of dough. Place braided loaves on cookie sheet and allow to rise for 1 more hour. Brush with egg yolk. Sprinkle with sugar. Bake at 350°F degrees for about 30 minutes.

Serves 4.

Source: "Foodista.com – The Cooking Encyclopedia Everyone Can Edit".`

Traditional Italian Pizzelle

A traditional Italian waffle cookie, generally served at Christmas, Easter, and at weddings.

INGREDIENTS:
6 eggs
1 1/2 cups sugar
1 cup melted margarine
2 tablespoons vanilla or anise flavor
3 1/2 cups flour
4 teaspoons baking powder

INSTRUCTIONS:
Beat eggs, and gradually add sugar. Add cooled margarine and flavor.

Sift flour and baking powder together, and stir into egg mixture.

Batter should be like a thick pancake batter, but if it is too thick, add about 1/4 cup milk to thin out.

Pizzelle iron should be hot. Brush with Crisco (occasionally). Drop 1 teaspoonful of batter into the center of each pattern of the iron, close cover, and cook between 30 and 45 seconds. Pizzelle should be a golden brown color. (Experiment with them to see how you like them, but they need to be cooked enough so they don't remain soft.)

Cool completely on wire rack before storing, as they get soggy if packed before cooled. Store in a foil-lined cookie tin for up to a month.

Source: "Foodista.com – The Cooking Encyclopedia Everyone Can Edit".

Miscellaneous

Beet Horseradish sauce

INGREDIENTS:
1 pound red beets, boiled
1 teaspoon salt
2 ounces horseradish, fresh
1 cup water
2 tablespoons vinegar
1 dash pepper
1 teaspoon sugar

INSTRUCTIONS:
Grate beets and horseradish. Combine vinegar, sugar, salt, pepper and water.

Bring to a boil. Pour over grated beets and horseradish. Mix thoroughly. Store in a covered jar in the refrigerator.

Source: "Foodista.com – The Cooking Encyclopedia Everyone Can Edit".

Chocolate Buttercream

INGREDIENTS:
1 cup butter or margarine, at room temperature
1/4 cup milk or heavy cream
2 teaspoons vanilla extract, or other desired flavoring
2 pounds confectioners' sugar
6 ounces semisweet chocolate, melted and cooled to lukewarm

INSTRUCTIONS:

Beat butter for a few seconds, simply to make it creamy. Add the milk and vanilla and beat on high speed until smooth, about 3 minutes. Add the chocolate and beat for 2 minutes. Add the sugar, one cup at a time, and beat on medium speed until all sugar is incorporated.

NOTE: To melt the chocolate, place it in a double boiler above simmering water. Remove from heat and let cool until lukewarm.

Chocolate Glaze

INGREDIENTS:
2 tablespoons cocoa
1 tablespoon corn syrup
1 tablespoon + 2 teaspoon water
1 tablespoon Crisco oil
1 cup confectioner's sugar, sift if lumpy

INSTRUCTIONS:
In a small saucepan combine all ingredients except sugar. Cook and stir over low heat until the mixture is smooth.

Remove from heat. Beat in sugar. If the mixture is too thick to pour easily, add a little more water.

Drizzle over cake.

Source: "Foodista.com – The Cooking Encyclopedia Everyone Can Edit".

Hard Cooked Easter Eggs

INGREDIENTS:
Eggs
1 tablespoon Vinegar
Water

INSTRUCTIONS:

Place eggs in a single layer saucepan.

Add enough water to come at least 1 inch above them.

Add a tablespoon of vinegar for better dye coverage after cooking.

Cover the pan and just quickly bring to boiling.

Turn off the heat. If necessary, remove the pan from the burner to prevent further boiling.

Let the eggs stand, covered, in the hot water for 15 minutes for large eggs, about 12 minutes for medium and 18 for extra-large eggs.

Immediately run cold water over the eggs or place them in ice water until completely cooled. Do not keep the eggs warm or at room temperature (between 40° and 140°F) for more than 2 hours.

Store in refrigerator until it's time to dye the eggs.

Source: "Foodista.com – The Cooking Encyclopedia Everyone Can Edit".

How to Dye Easter Eggs without Chemical Paints

How to Dye Easter Eggs without Chemical Paints

INGREDIENTS:
Eggs
1 tablespoon Vinegar
Water

Natural Products for the colors:
Light red, reddish purple - beets or blueberries
Golden orange - onion skins
Blue - Red cabbage leaves
Light Yellow - oranges or lemons rinds, carrots.
Yellow - the roots of turmeric, walnut shells
Light green - spinach leaves, nettle
Green - green apples

Beige or brown - coffee

INSTRUCTIONS:
Place the eggs in a saucepan, cover with water at least 1 inch above them. Add a teaspoon of vinegar. Boil eggs 15 minutes with natural coloring additives.

How to raise the dough

INSTRUCTIONS:
Method 1. In OVEN: Heat the oven for 2 or 3 minutes on 200°F just until it starts to get warm, not hot. Then place the dough in the warm oven to rise. Close the door.

Method 2. In MICROWAVE: If you have a big microwave, heat a glass of water for 1 minute then place the bowl of dough in the microwave with the hot glass of water and close the door.

Lemon Rice - side dish

Easy side dish

INGREDIENTS:
1 cup uncooked white rice
2 tablespoons butter or margarine
2 garlic cloves, minced
1 teaspoon grated lemon peel
1/4 teaspoon black pepper
2 cups chicken broth
2 tablespoons chopped fresh parsley

INSTRUCTIONS:
In a saucepan, put together all ingredients, except parsley. Bring the mixture to a boil.

Reduce heat, cover tightly, and simmer 15 minutes or until the liquid is absorbed and the rice is tender. Stir in parsley and serve.

Lemon Vinaigrette

INGREDIENTS:
1/2 cup olive oil
3 tablespoons fresh lemon juice
1 tablespoon minced shallot
1 1/2 teaspoons Dijon mustard
1/2 teaspoon grated lemon peel
1/2 teaspoon sugar

INSTRUCTIONS:
Combine all ingredients in a bowl and blend them. Salt and pepper.
Chill. Bring to room temperature before using. The Vinaigrette can be
prepared 1 day ahead.

Parmesan Mashed Potatoes

INGREDIENTS:
1 1/2 cups cream
1/4 teaspoon salt and pepper
2 pounds russet potatoes, peeled and cubed
1 stick Butter
1/4 cup Freshly grated parmesan cheese

INSTRUCTIONS:
Place potatoes in a medium pot and cover with cold water. Bring to a
boil, heat to a simmer. Add a generous pinch of salt and continue to
simmer until potatoes are fork tender, about 20 minutes. Heat cream, salt
and pepper and butter in a medium saucepan over medium heat until
steaming hot, about 6 minutes.

When potatoes are done, drain and return potatoes to pot to dry slightly.
Optional: Run potatoes through food mill or potato ricer into pot.

Add potatoes to the cream and butter mixture. Stir in parmesan cheese,
taste for seasoning.

Serves 4.

Philadelphia Mashed Potatoes - Easter side dish

INGREDIENTS:
6 cups peeled and quartered potatoes
1/2 cup milk
8 ounces cream cheese, softened
1/2 teaspoon onion powder
1/2 teaspoon salt
1/4 teaspoon pepper
1/4 teaspoons paprika

INSTRUCTIONS:
Place potatoes and enough water to cover in 3 quart saucepan. Bring to boil. Reduce heat to medium. Cook 20-25 minutes or until tender.

Drain. Mash potatoes, gradually stirring in milk, cream cheese, onion powder, salt and pepper until light and fluffy. Sprinkle with paprika. Serve immediately.

Yield: 8 servings.

Porcini Mushroom Stuffing

INGREDIENTS:
2 1/2 ounce packages dried porcini mushrooms
2 cups boiling water
2 tablespoons olive oil
1/2 pound crimini mushrooms, sliced
1/2 cup chopped shallots
1/2 cup chopped yellow onion
4 garlic cloves, chopped
5 cups ciabatta style bread, cubed
1 stick butter, melted

1 tablespoon fresh sage, minced
1 tablespoon fresh thyme, minced
2 teaspoons fresh rosemary, minced
Coarse salt
Cracked black pepper
1 large egg
1/2 cup grated Parmesan cheese
3 stalks celery, minced

INSTRUCTIONS:
Place porcini in a small bowl and pour 2 cups boiling water over. Let stand until soft, about 45 minutes. Drain and reserve soaking liquid. Chop porcini and set aside.

Heat large nonstick skillet over medium heat. Add olive oil. Add sliced crimini mushrooms. Saute until brown. Add porcini, shallots, celery and garlic. Reduce heat to medium-low; cover and stir occasionally, about 5 minutes.

Transfer mixture and any juices to large mixing bowl. Stir in bread cubes, butter, and fresh herbs into the mixture. Season with coarse salt and pepper. Mix in reserved porcini soaking liquid only until well coated, 1/4 cup at a time, not so it gets soggy. Cover and chill stuffing until ready to cook. The longer it marinated like this the better.

If chilled, bring stuffing to room temperature. Just before using, whisk egg to blend in small bowl and mix into stuffing. Mix in Parmesan cheese. Bake in a 350°F preheated oven until warmed fully, approximately 10 minutes.

Source: "Foodista.com – The Cooking Encyclopedia Everyone Can Edit".

Raspberry Vinegar

INGREDIENTS:
1 pint ripe raspberries
1 cup red wine vinegar

INSTRUCTIONS:

Put the whole raspberries in a clean jar. Add vinegar so it cover the berries. Cover the jar and let it stand at room temperature for 7 days.

Line a strainer with a double layer of cheesecloth and place the strainer over a bowl. Pour vinegar mixture. Gather corners of cheesecloth and squeeze the juices just until thicker juices begin to pass through the cheesecloth. Discard the cheesecloth. Bottle the vinegar. Cork and put in chill place up to 6 months.

Rhubarb Chutney

INGREDIENTS:
2 pounds fresh rhubarb, chopped
2 cups chopped onion
1-1/2 cups brown sugar
1 cup cider vinegar
2 teaspoon cinnamon
1 teaspoon ground ginger
1/2 teaspoon ground cloves
2 teaspoons salt

INSTRUCTIONS:
Put in large heavy saucepan: rhubarb, onion, brown sugar, vinegar, cinnamon, ginger, cloves, and salt. Cook until thickened (about 30 minutes). Stir often.

Put into hot sterilized jars. Cover with canning lids. Set aside to cool and seal.

Yield: 2 pints

Seafood Dip

INGREDIENTS:
1 (8-ounce) container sour cream
1 cup chopped cooked shrimp or crabmeat
1/3 cup finely chopped green pepper
1/3 cup finely chopped onion
1/3 cup finely chopped celery

1/3 cup bottled chili sauce
1 tablespoon horseradish

INSTRUCTIONS:
In a large bowl, combine all ingredients. Stir well and chill. Keep in the refrigerator until ready to serve.

Tartar Sauce #1

INGREDIENTS:
1 small onion, chopped fine
1 cup mayonnaise
1 cup chopped cucumber pickles
2 tablespoons Parsley, finely chopped

INSTRUCTIONS:
Mix onion, cucumber pickles, parsley and mayonnaise. Stir and serve or refrigerate for later use.

Tartar Sauce #2

INGREDIENTS:
1/2 teaspoon mustard
1 teaspoon powdered sugar
1/2 teaspoon salt
cayenne few grains
2 eggs Yolks
1/2 cup olive oil
1 1/2 tablespoons vinegar

1/2 tablespoon capers finely chopped
1/2 tablespoon Pickles finely chopped
1/2 tablespoon Olives finely chopped
Parsley
1/2 shallot, finely chopped
1/4 teaspoon powdered tarragon or 1 tablespoon tarragon vinegar

INSTRUCTIONS:

Mix mustard, sugar, salt, and cayenne. Add yolks of eggs, and stir until thoroughly mixed, setting the bowl in a pan of ice-water. Add oil, at first drop by drop, stirring with a wooden spoon or wire whisk. As the mixture thickens, dilute with vinegar, when oil may be added more rapidly.

Keep in a cool place until ready to serve, then add the remaining ingredients.

Printed in Great Britain
by Amazon